ISOLATION
JOURNAL

QUESTIONS TO HELP YOU DOCUMENT, PROCESS, AND FLOURISH DURING SELF ISOLATION AND COVID-19.

BY LEILA CHALK

&

(WRITE YOUR NAME HERE)

ISOLATION

JOURNAL

COPYRIGHT LEILA CHALK 2020
ACKNOWLEDGEMENT FOR ALL THE GREAT ARTISTS WHOSE
DESIGNS MADE THIS WORK POSSIBLE.

how to use this journal

AND FEEL BETTER DOING IT

questions

there are questions in this journal. use them as a springboard for your daily contemplation.

suggestions

there are prompts and suggestions on how to stay connected during social distancing.

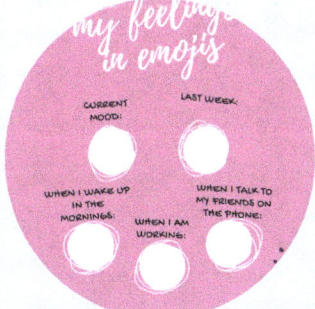

check ins

there are pages with very structured tasks to help you get unstuck when things are really messy.

ready. set. go!

WHY ARE YOU ISOLATING?

WRITE IT DOWN

It is important to think about the purpose of the things we do, so that we can drill down into our needs and desires. Why are you isolating? It may help to talk to a friend or your therapist about this.

FRIENDS
are the family we choose.

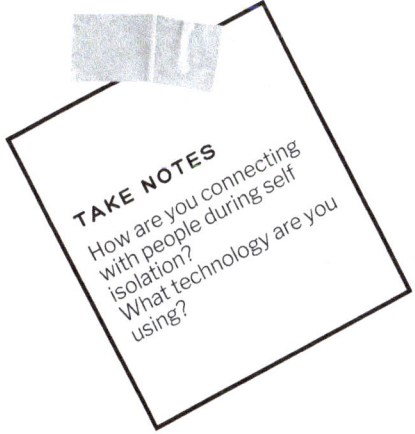

TAKE NOTES
How are you connecting with people during self isolation? What technology are you using?

QUICK 6
CHECK IN WITH YOURSELF

MORNING

HOW ARE YOU FEELING?

WHAT ARE YOUR GOALS?

AFTERNOON

WHAT DID YOU EAT TODAY?

HOW DOES YOUR BODY FEEL?

EVENING

WHAT HAPPENED OUTSIDE IN THE WORLD?

WHAT IS YOUR BED TIME ROUTINE?

1 - 5, RATE YOUR MINDSET. _____

WHAT IS SOMETHING THAT IS HAPPENING
IN YOUR TOWN RIGHT NOW?

**LOCATION
LOCATION
LOCATION**

Different parts of the world are experiencing COVID-19 differently. Write down something that is specific to where you live.
How is it making you feel?

FIVE THINGS
I'm Thankful For

1.

2.

3.

4.

5.

In a world full of chaos, ground yourself with the beautiful things going in your life.

WRITE A HAIKU
ABOUT YOUR TIME IN ISO

How are you feeling today?

WRITE DOWN HOW YOU FEEL AND THEN COLOUR ME IN

WHO IS IN YOUR ISOLATION TEAM?

my feelings in emojis

CURRENT MOOD:

LAST WEEK:

WHEN I WAKE UP IN THE MORNINGS:

WHEN I AM WORKING:

WHEN I TALK TO MY FRIENDS ON THE PHONE:

DRAW YOUR EMOJIS WHEN YOU ARE UNABLE TO USE YOUR WORDS.
#ISOYOURNAL

WHAT DO YOU MISS THE MOST FROM YOUR PRE-ISO LIFE?

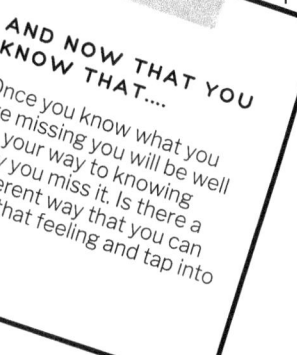

AND NOW THAT YOU KNOW THAT....

Once you know what you're missing you will be well on your way to knowing why you miss it. Is there a different way that you can get that feeling and tap into it?

How are you feeling today?

ART IN PROGRESS

DOODLE SOMETHING. STICK FIGURES ARE OK. #ISOJOURNAL

today I Will ...

WHAT IS YOUR TO-DO LIST FOR TODAY?. #ISOJOURNAL

WHAT ARE YOU AFRAID OF?

WRITE IT DOWN

Being able to write down what you are afraid of will help you face those feelings.
Dot points, brain mapping, hieroglyphs. However you want to process it, that's ok.

TALKING POINTS

It may help to use this page to speak to a friend or counselor, too.

Reflective Essay Writing

There is a reason they kept teaching us how to write reflective and introspective pieces. Write a short reflective essay on the moments when you felt the most alive.

YAY!
WHAT IS SOMETHING THAT HAS MADE YOU HAPPY TODAY?

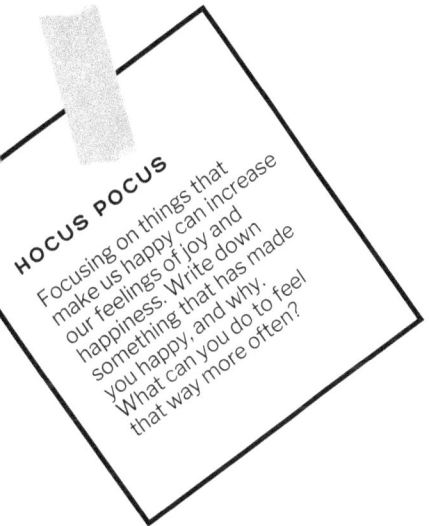

HOCUS POCUS

Focusing on things that make us happy can increase our feelings of joy and happiness. Write down something that has made you happy, and why. What can you do to feel that way more often?

WHAT IS SOMETHING THAT HAS MADE YOU
CRY?

TEARS ARE OK, TOO

When was the last time you cried? What made you feel that way?
How did you feel after?

How are you feeling today?

SELF-CARE BINGO

TOOK A SHOWER	GOT DRESSED	CAUGHT UP WITH FRIENDS	PROCESSED MY FEELINGS	COMPLIMENTED MYSELF
MEDITATED	ATE GOOD FOOD	LISTENED TO MY BODY	HAD FUN	ASKED FOR HELP
TOOK A MUCH-NEEDED BREAK	DRANK WATER	*Free*	TAKE A SOCIAL MEDIA BREAK	TREATED MYSELF
COMPLIMENTED SOMEONE	GOT 8 HOURS OF SLEEP	TOOK STEPS TO TAME NEGATIVE THOUGHTS	DIDN'T HUG MY PARENTS	DROPPED A HABIT THAT IS NOT FOR ME
TOOK A MENTAL HEALTH DAY	SPENDING TIME WITH NATURE	DECLUTTERED MY SPACE	WROTE DOWN IN MY JOURNAL	PRACTICED SELF-COMPASSION

WHERE ARE YOU ISOLATING?
DESCRIBE YOUR SPACE

LOVE YOUR CRAFT

DO SOMETHING CREATIVE

And then write about it here! What is something creative you have done today? How did it make you feel?

QUICK 6
CHECK IN WITH YOURSELF

MORNING

HOW ARE YOU FEELING?

WHAT ARE YOUR GOALS?

AFTERNOON

WHAT DID YOU EAT TODAY?

HOW DOES YOUR BODY FEEL?

EVENING

WHAT HAPPENED OUTSIDE IN THE WORLD?

WHAT IS YOUR BED TIME ROUTINE?

1 - 5, RATE YOUR MINDSET. _____

WRITE A STORY ABOUT YOUR FAMILY BUT REFER TO THEM AS YOUR COWORKERS

READ IT OUT LOUD
Consider reading the story to the fam-bam.

OLD SCHOOL BOOK REPORT
YES, YES, READ A BOOK, WRITE A REPORT.

Book Title:
Author:

Setting of the story:	Main characters:

Summary of plot:	Challenges faced by the main characters:

Climax or defining moment of the story:	Ending of the story:

Lessons learned:	Comments and observations:

WHAT NEW SKILLS HAVE YOU DEVELOPED WHILE IN ISOLATION?

NO PRESSURE

We sometimes put too much pressure on ourselves to develop new skills. This isn't that. Chances are, you've had to learn how to do something in a very new way. Write about it here.

WHAT IS SOMETHING THAT IS HELPING YOU STAY POSITIVE?

WHAT GOVERNMENT REGULATIONS ARE IN PLACE AND HOW DO THEY MAKE YOU FEEL?

LAW AND ORDER

The law has a very large role to play in our every day lives. We interact with it unthinkingly all the time. Now, we are often having to think about fast changing regulations. What are they in your town and how do they make you feel?

QUICK QUCIK QUICK
TELL SOMEONE YOU LOVE THEM.

How are you feeling today?

How are you feeling today?

QUICK 6

WRITE A SENTENCE ABOUT YOUR DAY

WHAT IS IN THE NEWS?

HOW DID YOU FEEL WHEN YOU WOKE UP?

WHAT DID YOU EAT AND DRINK TODAY?

WHAT IS SOMETHING YOU ARE CONCERNED ABOUT?

WHO DID YOU SPEAK TO TODAY? WHAT DID YOU SAY?

WHAT IS SOMETHING YOU ARE GRATEFUL FOR?

NETFLIX AND ???

WHAT IS SOMETHING YOU ARE WATCHING NOW?

WRITE ABOUT THE MEDIA YOU ARE CONSUMING

and how it makes you feel? Do you feel like you are living in a movie? Describe it.

CREATE A PLAY LIST
AND SEND IT TO A FRIEND

MIX TAPES ARE COOL

LEAVE YOUR MARK - WHAT IS YOUR ISO #TAG?

How are you feeling today?

DID YOU PANIC BUY?

AND WHY?
Everyone else did, did you?
You are only human.
Describe your feelings here.

MEDITATE FOR ONE MINUTE TODAY.
TWO MINUTES TOMORROW.
FOUR MINUTES THE DAY AFTER THAT.

HOW ARE YOU CONNECTING WITH THE PEOPLE AROUND YOU?

BLOG WRITING PROMPT - CONTRIBUTE SOMETHING ONLINE

Name:

Date:

Topic:

Published: Yes / No

Music. Art. Therapy. Discuss in the four boxes below how they are related and how they impact your life in insolation. This is to be shared with other people, which changes how you write. Post a link with the #isojournal on your Facebook or Blog.

COLOUR ME HAPPY

#ISOJOURNAL

QUICK 6
CHECK IN WITH YOURSELF

MORNING

HOW ARE YOU FEELING?

WHAT ARE YOUR GOALS?

AFTERNOON

WHAT DID YOU EAT TODAY?

HOW DOES YOUR BODY FEEL?

EVENING

WHAT HAPPENED OUTSIDE IN THE WORLD?

WHAT IS YOUR BED TIME ROUTINE?

1 - 5, RATE YOUR MINDSET. _____

QUICK 6

CHECK IN WITH YOURSELF

MORNING	AFTERNOON	EVENING
HOW ARE YOU FEELING?	WHAT DID YOU EAT TODAY?	WHAT HAPPENED OUTSIDE IN THE WORLD?
WHAT ARE YOUR GOALS?	HOW DOES YOUR BODY FEEL?	WHAT IS YOUR BED TIME ROUTINE?

1 - 5, RATE YOUR MINDSET. _____

WHAT IS SOMETHING THAT THE NEWS ARE REPORTING ON NOW AND HOW DO YOU FEEL?

WHAT HAS CHANGED
ABOUT YOUR JOB?

quick six
DRAWING EDITION

CURRENT MOOD

FAVE FLOWER

SPIRIT ANIMAL

FAVE PERSON

WEATHER OUTSIDE

MY FAM BAM

QUICK 6

what happened today?

How is your inner child feeling?

Involve the family - how are they coping today?

What is something you learned today?

What resources do you rely on?

Did you take a break today?

If you stretched, could you touch your toes?

WHAT IS THE BIGGEST DIFFERENCE IN
HOW YOU SPEND YOUR DAYS?

How are you feeling today?

YES YOU CAN

DRAW SOMETHING THAT YOU CAN THEN EITHER SCAN AND POST ON LINE WITH THE #ISOJOURNAL TAG...

OR MAIL TO YOUR PARENTS SO THEY CAN PUT IT ON THEIR FRIDGE. HA!

WHAT DO YOU THINK THE WORLD WILL LOOK LIKE
WHEN ALL THIS IS OVER?

How are you feeling today?

Your feelings are valid.

How are you feeling today?

KEEPING FIT
WHAT EXERCISE ARE YOU DOING?

HOW DOES IT MAKE YOU FEEL?

Exercise speaks for itself. You don't need your journal telling you that you should do it. Start small. Plan it out. Talk to people about it. We are all in this together.

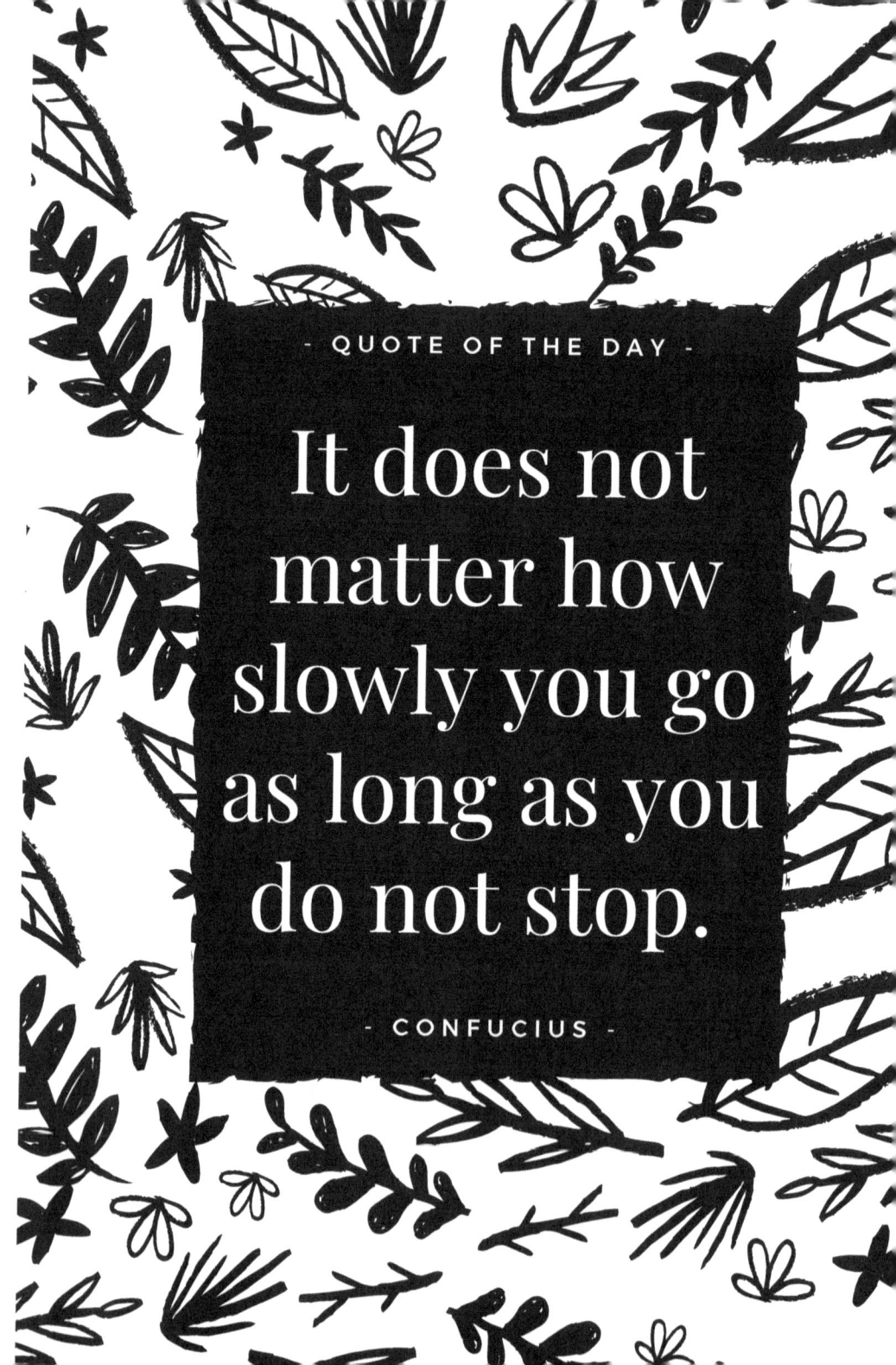

WHAT IS HAPPENING IN
YOUR FAVOURITE PLACE?

THE WORLD IS BEAUTIFUL
What is going on in your global village?

WRITE A LETTER
TO YOURSELF FIVE YEARS FROM NOW

USE SOCIAL MEDIA TO BE SOCIAL!
STOP SCROLLING - GET IN TOUCH WITH PEOPLE.

MIND MAP
MAP OUT HOW YOU ARE FEELING TODAY

BE A CHILD TODAY

1. Make your favourite childhood breakfast.

2. Skip rope. Do your favourite childhood exercise.

3. Quiet time: Reading
   Puzzles and/or colouring in activity

4. Make a creative bento box lunch from leftovers.

5. Read about dinosaurs on wikipedia.

6. Download an online crossword to do.

7. Consider a nap.

8. Art activity: Draw your favorite animal

How are you feeling today?

BRAINSTORM YOUR NEXT HOLIDAY
DOT POINTS ONLY

WRITE A LIST OF
QUESTIONS YOU ARE STRUGGLING WITH

YOU DON'T HAVE TO ANSWER THEM

Sometimes knowing what you don't know is the first place to start in any journey of self discovery. Start here.

POETRY
IN ISOLATION

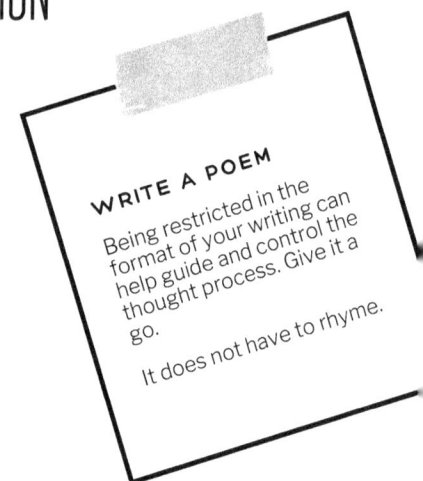

WRITE A POEM

Being restricted in the format of your writing can help guide and control the thought process. Give it a go.

It does not have to rhyme.

How are you feeling today?

WHO DO YOU MISS?

TAKE NOTES

There are wonderful people in your life. You may not have their number.

How are you feeling today?

all about my current faves

1 MY CURRENT FAVOURITE SNACK:

2 MY CURRENT FAVOURITE TV SHOW:

3 MY CURRENT FAVOURITE PODCAST:

4 MY CURRENT FAVOURITE RESTAURANT:

5 MY CURRENT STYLE:

How are you feeling today?

DESCRIBE YOUR FAVOURITE PARK
FEEL - SEE - SMELL - HEAR - TASTE - TOUCH

MEDITATION

If you have a favourite outdoor space, imagine it now. The further away from you it is, the better. Describe in detail the image including things you would feel, see, smell, hear, taste, and touch.

HOW TO CONNECT

ONE FRIEND YOU WILL CALL THIS WEEK?

WHO HAVE YOU SCHEDULED AN E-COFFEE WITH?

IS THERE A SCHOOL FRIEND YOU THINK MAY BE STRUGGLING?

FAMILY MEMBER NEEDING AN E-HUG?

WHAT ARE YOU FEELING? SINGLE WORDS ONLY.

WHAT ARE YOU FEELING? PICTURES ONLY.

HISTORY LESSON FOR THE FUTURE
PRETEND IT'S 2060

PRETEND IT'S 2060

Or some other year that works for you. What do you think the next generation is going to learn from this moment in history? How does that make you feel?

Comfy White Tee

FAVE OUTFIT

Describe your favourite iSO outfit.

How are you feeling today?

CREATIVE WRITING EXERCISE
WHICH DINOSAUR WOULD DO BEST IN ISO?

SOME THINGS WILL NEVER CHANGE

WRITE WHAT YOU HOPE WILL ALWAYS BE JUST LIKE THIS.

JOURNAL IT
It is ok to feel like some things in isolation are nice. Write them down. Explore why they feel good.

MOVEMENT

FITNESS PLAN

WEEK # ___

COPY AS NEEDED

DAY 1 | MON

DAY 2 | TUE

DAY 3 | WED

DAY 4 | THU

DAY 5 | FRI

REMEMBER ME!
WHAT DO YOU WANT TO REMEMBER ABOUT THIS MOMENT IN YOUR LIFE?

How are you feeling today?

DRAW YOUR DAY
WHILE IN ISOLATION.

How are you feeling today?

TODAY YOU ARE AN INVENTOR.
INVENT SOMETHING THAT WOULD MAKE YOUR LIFE EASIER.

How are you feeling today?

How are you feeling today?

FIVE THINGS

I'm Thankful For

1.

2.

3.

4.

5.

How are you feeling today?

MESSAGES
WHAT DO YOU WANT TO SAY?

SELF-CARE BINGO - PLAY AGAIN

TOOK A SHOWER	GOT DRESSED	CAUGHT UP WITH FRIENDS	PROCESSED MY FEELINGS	COMPLIMENTED MYSELF
MEDITATED	ATE GOOD FOOD	LISTENED TO MY BODY	HAD FUN	ASKED FOR HELP
TOOK A MUCH-NEEDED BREAK	DRANK WATER	*Free*	TAKE A SOCIAL MEDIA BREAK	TREATED MYSELF
COMPLIMENTED SOMEONE	GOT 8 HOURS OF SLEEP	TOOK STEPS TO TAME NEGATIVE THOUGHTS	DIDN'T HUG MY PARENTS	DROPPED A HABIT THAT IS NOT FOR ME
TOOK A MENTAL HEALTH DAY	SPENDING TIME WITH NATURE	DECLUTTERED MY SPACE	WROTE DOWN IN MY JOURNAL	PRACTICED SELF-COMPASSION

How are you feeling today?

WRITE A STORY ABOUT YOUR PETS BUT REFER TO THEM
AS YOUR COWORKERS

READ IT OUT LOUD
Consider reading the sto[ry]
to the fam-bam.

QUICK 6

CHECK IN WITH YOURSELF

MORNING	AFTERNOON	EVENING
HOW ARE YOU FEELING?	WHAT DID YOU EAT TODAY?	WHAT HAPPENED OUTSIDE IN THE WORLD?
WHAT ARE YOUR GOALS?	HOW DOES YOUR BODY FEEL?	WHAT IS YOUR BED TIME ROUTINE?

1 - 5, RATE YOUR MINDSET. _____

How are you feeling today?

How are you feeling today?

WHAT TECH IS WORKING FOR YOU
WHILE IN ISOLATION?

WHAT IS SOMETHING YOU WANT TO LEARN?

Write down a plan to tackle it today.

How are you feeling today?

QUICK 6

WRITE A SENTENCE ABOUT YOUR DAY

WHAT IS IN THE NEWS?

HOW DID YOU FEEL WHEN YOU WOKE UP?

WHAT DID YOU EAT AND DRINK TODAY?

WHAT IS SOMETHING YOU ARE CONCERNED ABOUT?

WHO DID YOU SPEAK TO TODAY? WHAT DID YOU SAY?

WHAT IS SOMETHING YOU ARE GRATEFUL FOR?

Do you have a morning routine?
What is it?

How are you feeling today?

How are you feeling today?

How are you feeling today?

PLOT TWIST

HOW WOULD COVID-19 IMPACT
YOUR FAVOURITE TV SHOW?

SOMETHING POSITIVE ABOUT YOUR DAY
WRITE IT DOWN.

MINDFULNESS

DOODLE YOUR THOUGHTS

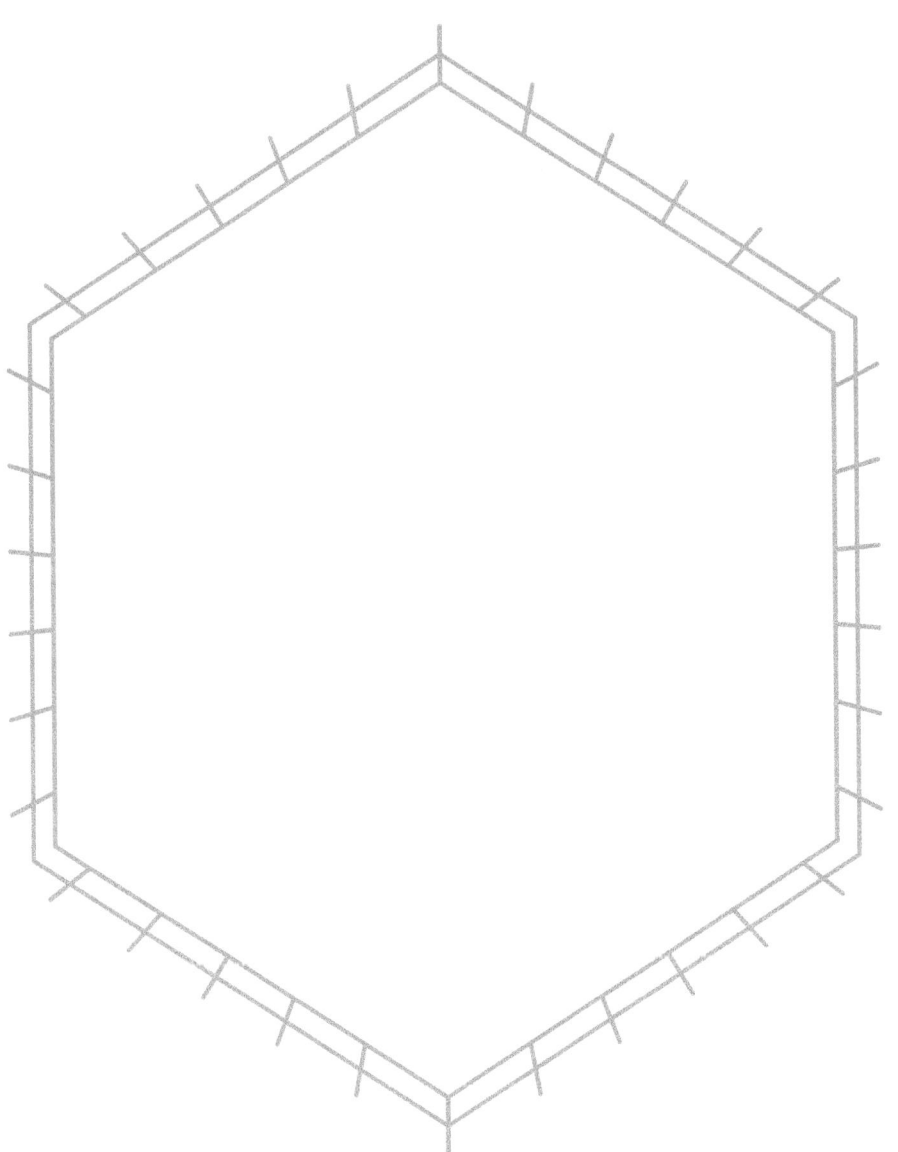

How are you feeling today?

FIND A WAY TO BE CREATIVE TODAY.
FIND A WAY TO BUILD SOMETHING.

PLAY WITH LEGO (OR BLOCKS)

HOW ARE YOU GETTING YOUR FOOD?
AND WHAT ARE YOU EATING?

INSTANT MESSAGING IS NICE, BUT, ALSO
SEND AN EMAIL TO A FRIEND.

QUICK 6
CHECK IN WITH YOURSELF

MORNING

HOW ARE YOU FEELING?

WHAT ARE YOUR GOALS?

AFTERNOON

WHAT DID YOU EAT TODAY?

HOW DOES YOUR BODY FEEL?

EVENING

WHAT HAPPENED OUTSIDE IN THE WORLD?

WHAT IS YOUR BED TIME ROUTINE?

1 - 5, RATE YOUR MINDSET. _____

Hello
SELF

How are you feeling today?

QUICK 6
CHECK IN WITH YOURSELF

MORNING

HOW ARE YOU FEELING?

WHAT ARE YOUR GOALS?

AFTERNOON

WHAT DID YOU EAT TODAY?

HOW DOES YOUR BODY FEEL?

EVENING

WHAT HAPPENED OUTSIDE IN THE WORLD?

WHAT IS YOUR BED TIME ROUTINE?

1 - 5, RATE YOUR MINDSET. _____

BAD JOKES

HAVE YOU HEARD ANY BAD ISO JOKES?

Did they make you laugh?

CREATIVE WRITING

HOW ARE THESE PEOPLE TACKLING ISO?

How are you feeling today?

go play hopscotch.
write about it here.

QUICK 6
CHECK IN WITH YOURSELF

MORNING	AFTERNOON	EVENING
HOW ARE YOU FEELING?	WHAT DID YOU EAT TODAY?	WHAT HAPPENED OUTSIDE IN THE WORLD?
WHAT ARE YOUR GOALS?	HOW DOES YOUR BODY FEEL?	WHAT IS YOUR BED TIME ROUTINE?

1 - 5, RATE YOUR MINDSET. _____

WHAT IS THE MOST SHOCKING CONVERSATION YOU HAVE HAD?

QUICK 6
CHECK IN WITH YOURSELF

MORNING

HOW ARE YOU FEELING?

WHAT ARE YOUR GOALS?

AFTERNOON

WHAT DID YOU EAT TODAY?

HOW DOES YOUR BODY FEEL?

EVENING

WHAT HAPPENED OUTSIDE IN THE WORLD?

WHAT IS YOUR BED TIME ROUTINE?

1 - 5, RATE YOUR MINDSET. _____

How are you feeling today?

How are you feeling today?

How are you feeling today?

QUICK 6
CHECK IN WITH YOURSELF

MORNING

HOW ARE YOU FEELING?

WHAT ARE YOUR GOALS?

AFTERNOON

WHAT DID YOU EAT TODAY?

HOW DOES YOUR BODY FEEL?

EVENING

WHAT HAPPENED OUTSIDE IN THE WORLD?

WHAT IS YOUR BED TIME ROUTINE?

1 - 5, RATE YOUR MINDSET. _____

WHAT BOOKS ARE YOU READING?

How are you feeling today?

QUICK 6

what happened today?

How is your inner child feeling?

Involve the family - how are they coping today?

What is something you learned today?

What resources do you rely on?

Did you take a break today?

If you stretched, could you touch your toes?

How are you feeling today?

How are you feeling today?

CREATE AN AT HOME CAFE
AND DESIGN A MENU FOR YOUR ISO-TEAM.

How are you feeling today?

How are you feeling today?

How are you feeling today?

MESSAGES
WHAT DO YOU WANT TO SAY?

SELF-CARE BINGO - PLAY AGAIN

TOOK A SHOWER	GOT DRESSED	CAUGHT UP WITH FRIENDS	PROCESSED MY FEELINGS	COMPLIMENTED MYSELF
MEDITATED	ATE GOOD FOOD	LISTENED TO MY BODY	HAD FUN	ASKED FOR HELP
TOOK A MUCH-NEEDED BREAK	DRANK WATER	*Free*	TAKE A SOCIAL MEDIA BREAK	TREATED MYSELF
COMPLIMENTED SOMEONE	GOT 8 HOURS OF SLEEP	TOOK STEPS TO TAME NEGATIVE THOUGHTS	DIDN'T HUG MY PARENTS	DROPPED A HABIT THAT IS NOT FOR ME
TOOK A MENTAL HEALTH DAY	SPENDING TIME WITH NATURE	DECLUTTERED MY SPACE	WROTE DOWN IN MY JOURNAL	PRACTICED SELF-COMPASSION

MINDFULNESS
DOODLE YOUR THOUGHTS

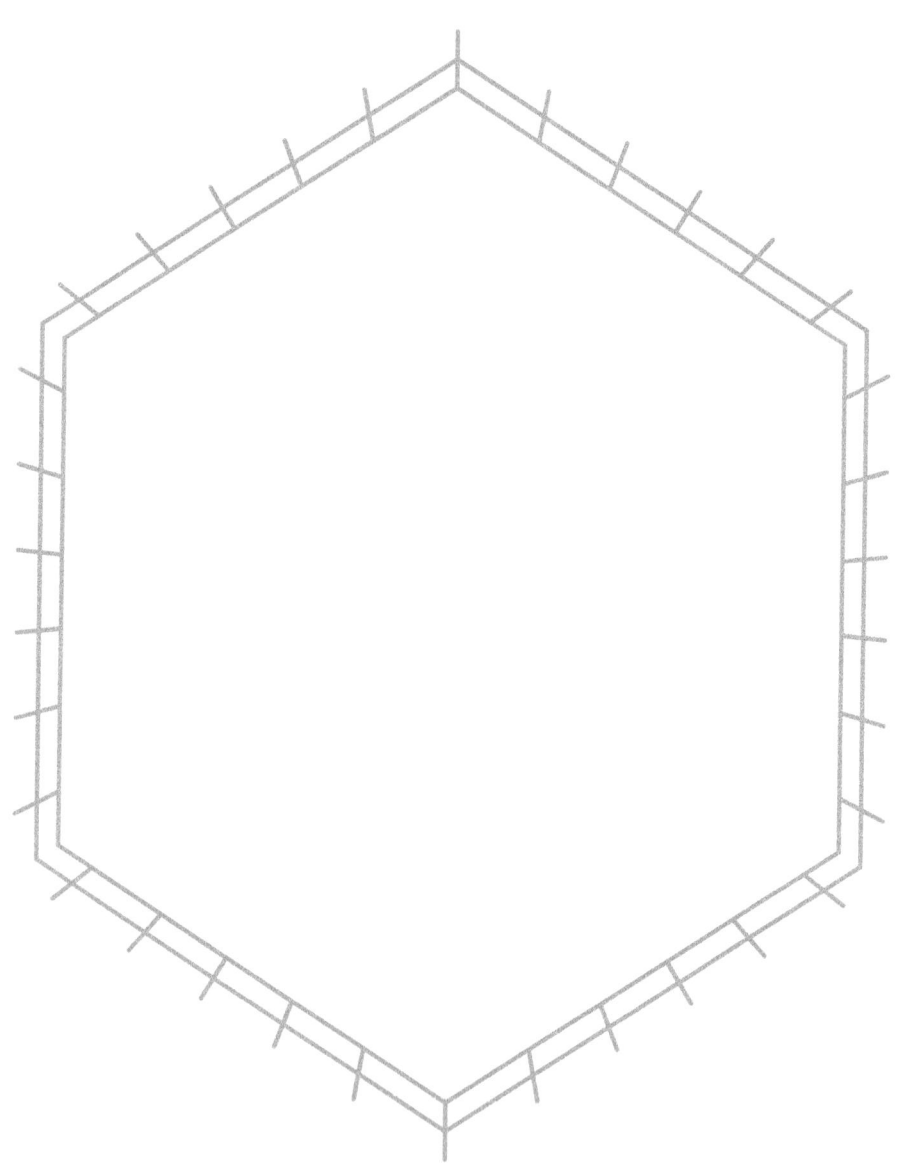

How are you feeling today?

How are you feeling today?

QUICK 6

CHECK IN WITH YOURSELF

MORNING	AFTERNOON	EVENING
HOW ARE YOU FEELING?	WHAT DID YOU EAT TODAY?	WHAT HAPPENED OUTSIDE IN THE WORLD?
WHAT ARE YOUR GOALS?	HOW DOES YOUR BODY FEEL?	WHAT IS YOUR BED TIME ROUTINE?

1 - 5, RATE YOUR MINDSET. _____

How are you feeling today?

TRY TO MAKE FOUR PHONE CALLS TODAY,
JUST TO CHECK IN.

IT CAN BE HARD TO KNOW WHAT TO TALK
ABOUT WHEN EVERYONE IS GRIEVING.
WRITE AN AGENDA, YOUR FRIENDS WILL BE
GRATEFUL, TOO.

How are you feeling today?

QUICK 6
CHECK IN WITH YOURSELF

MORNING

HOW ARE YOU FEELING?

WHAT ARE YOUR GOALS?

AFTERNOON

WHAT DID YOU EAT TODAY?

HOW DOES YOUR BODY FEEL?

EVENING

WHAT HAPPENED OUTSIDE IN THE WORLD?

WHAT IS YOUR BED TIME ROUTINE?

1 - 5, RATE YOUR MINDSET. _____

www.ingramcontent.com/pod-product-compliance
Lightning Source LLC
Chambersburg PA
CBHW050312010526
44107CB00055B/2206